I0028393

Sidney Korshak

How to Land a
Legal Job Overseas

Andalus Publishing 2014

Landing a Legal Job Overseas
©2014 Andalus Publishing
ISBN-13: 978-0-9910476-5-9
All rights reserved. No part of this publication may be
produced or transmitted in any form or by any means,
electronic or mechanical, including photocopying recording
or any information storage and retrieval system, without the
prior written permission of the publisher. For permissions
contact: admin@andaluspublishing.com.

Publisher's Cataloging-In-Publication Data

Korshak, Sydney.
    How to land a legal job overseas / Sidney Korshak.
    Chicago : Andalus Publishing, c2014.

    p. ; cm.

    Includes index.
    ISBN: 978-0-9910476-5-9

    Summary: A guide to finding a job in the legal profession outside the United
States. The book contains a brief background on the groundbreaking American
lawyers who practiced outside the United States. It also contains job-hunting advice of a general nature, including tips on how to get experience without previous
employment. –Publisher.

    1. Law–Vocational guidance–Handbooks, manuals,etc. 2. Lawyers–
Employment–Foreign countries–Handbooks, manuals, etc. 3. Employment in
foreign countries–Handbooks, manuals, etc. 4. Americans–Employment–Foreign
countries–Handbooks, manuals, etc. 5. Job hunting–Foreign countries–Handbooks,
manuals, etc. I. Title.

KF297.K67 2014

340.023–dc23   2015

Contents

Chapter 1

INTRODUCTION

WHY THIS BOOK?

Over the past several years I have frequently received inquiries from lawyers interested in working in the Middle East. Usually these lawyers have American legal degrees and wish to explore employment options outside the United States. I have tried to respond to these inquiries whenever I could do so. Older lawyers have a responsibility to younger members of the bar. All of us can remember those who helped when we were starting out and it is only fair that we return the favor. Because of these inquiries, I thought that perhaps it would be useful to collect and compile the advice I have given and make it available to a wider audience and not simply those who

3

crossed paths with me professionally.

I have also looked around the Internet and found that the readily available materials for the attorney foreign job-seeker to be inadequate. Generally speaking, law schools barely acknowledge the fact that law is an international business and while many are successful in placing graduates locally, many have a more difficult time placing graduates overseas. This book, written from a commercial bias, is designed to fill the gap.

There is no "one size fits all" method for finding a position as a lawyer outside the United States. These methods have worked for me and they have worked for many others. The tips I share have saved me time and I trust they will save you time as well. My focus is on the recent American-trained graduate, but more experienced lawyers looking to make a career move might benefit from these methods as well.

A law graduate who wished to work as a lawyer overseas formerly had limited options. It was not that long ago that the Supreme Court struck U.S. citizenship as a requirement for the practice of law, but most countries will still only grant law licenses to their own nationals. Perhaps because job-seeking law students are necessarily focused on the requirements they must meet for bar admission, as they must be, they similarly focus on bar admission rules in foreign countries. Citizenship, language, different legal systems and additional required years of study all conspire to create daunting requirements. Students reach the conclusion that foreign bar admission is beyond their reach and so quickly give up. But not everyone sees it this way, and crucially, not everyone saw it this way.

In the 1920's Russell Baker rode the rails from New Mexico to Chicago to begin his law studies. The partnership he began with Chicago litigator Jack McKenzie eventually grew into the United States' first truly international law firm. That firm, known as Baker & McKenzie, today has offices is forty-seven countries around the world. But when Baker started out, he had only an office on Washington Street in Chicago. There were no out of state or foreign offices. Jack McKenzie had a rather typical local litigation practice, focusing on insurance defense work. The firm's first foreign office was the result of a merger with a firm in Caracas, Venezuela. Illinois at the time had an innovative rule that allowed foreign lawyers to become members of an Illinois law partnership even though they were not admitted to practice in the state. The Venezuelan attorneys became members of the Chicago partnership and from there the firm took off. Though Baker tried to convince lawyers in other countries to join his firm, he was not always successful in convincing foreign firms to merge with his Illinois firm and so the firm began to establish foreign offices itself. Licensing was an issue. These American attorneys did not have foreign licenses and could not appear as attorneys in foreign courts. So in its early years, Baker and McKenzie attorneys overseas worked as journalists or consultants. Their visas contained no mention of their status as American attorneys, and yet many had long and successful careers overseas. This technique pioneered by the firm is still used today.

Russell Baker was not the first American lawyer to practice overseas. Other Americans preceded him. Other American lawyers had already gone to Panama, the Philippines, Cuba, Puerto Rico and even China. Norwood Allman was a former State Department employee who went into private practice in Shanghai where there was a now forgotten United States District Court for Shanghai. His book, *Shanghai Lawyer*, published in 1943, is required reading for any lawyer interested in practicing overseas.

Unfortunately, the Shanghai District Court–one of perhaps only two or three in our history that have closed–was shuttered in 1940 when Japan finally moved troops into Shanghai. The closing of the court became permanent because there was no effort to re-establish the foreign settlements in China after World War II. In 1949, the People's Republic came to power and the idea of an American court in China became preposterous.

The idea of the overseas practice of law

was never as established in the United States as it was in Britain. An attorney called to the bar in London can be admitted and practice in the courts of many former British colonies around the world. The British colonial experience created a tradition of attorneys going abroad, a tradition that American attorneys simply do not share. Fortunately, all is not lost and there are many positions open overseas for American attorneys today. Even though the United States District Court in Shanghai will never re-open, there are once again American lawyers working in China.

Chapter 2

WHY WORK OVERSEAS?

WHY WORK OVERSEAS? IF YOU HAVE always been interested in international work and are looking for something outside the norm, an overseas position may be for you. If you don't mind being pulled out of your comfort zone and can tolerate—or thrive in—foreign cultures, perhaps an attorney position overseas is for you.

Another reason may be because attorney positions on offer in the United States are not satisfying. Did you spend three years of your life so that you could dedicate the rest of it to automobile accidents? Or products that failed? Or, as one movie attorney portrayed in *The Big Chill* said after dedicating her life to public service as a public defender, "I didn't realize they would be so guilty?" Or perhaps your 60+ plus hour per week *The Paper Chase* dream job is financially rewarding but the only day you are happy is the day you receive your check.   Meanwhile, you measure the rest of your days by the relationships deteriorating around you.   Divorce, heretofore unthinkable, now becomes inevitable.   Perhaps you are discouraged because the jobs you have been offered are not exactly the job you've worked so hard for. Or perhaps you want to strike out for adventure. Or perhaps a spouse has been transferred overseas and you are afraid that you will not be able to practice law anymore.   There are many reasons for going.

Practicing in a foreign country is not for everyone.   There is a reason the U.S. State Department classifies some countries as hardship posts. Some individuals fail to tolerate foreign postings well. I have seen a lawyer eat himself into a hospital because he could not admit to himself that his transfer to a foreign country was a failure. His newly acquired eating disorder was his ticket home. For others, being surrounded by a foreign language is disorienting and the principles of an unfamiliar legal system challenging. A legal system that defines a contract as a combination of offer and acceptance based on consideration can seem so comforting. But so far away.

Not being able to speak a foreign language should present no major difficulties. English is the lingua franca of the international legal world. English is the language of international business and often even of government. The ability to speak the local language will not necessarily be a job qualification. While the inability to speak the local language will impact your job prospects from jurisdiction to jurisdiction, you will find surprisingly few practical limitations as a candidate. You will find, though, that many positions in China require proficiency in Mandarin.

As a native speaker of English who has been exposed to legal vocabulary, you are in a position to correct documents for those who are not native speakers. For example, if the Saudis want an Arabic speaker, they do not typically look to foreign countries to find one when there are already competent candidates among their own population. What a foreign employer wants from you is your competence in both the law and in English.

Working overseas can be rewarding. You may find yourself working at young age at a level of practice you could not possibly have dreamed of. I have always felt that the Supreme Court decision permitting lawyer advertising was a mistake that ultimately has led to the decay of the profession. Once I was given the task of recommending rules for the regulation of attorneys in an overseas jurisdiction. Of course, I included a provision prohibiting advertising by attorneys. Overruling the Supreme Court is something few attorneys ever get the chance to do.

If you are reading this book and you don't have a law degree, much of the advice here can also apply to paralegal professionals. In many countries, the study of law leads only to an undergraduate degree. In the United Kingdom, because law is an undergraduate degree, recent graduates go right to work for law firms where they work for two years before taking the qualifying exam. This is why you see "PQE" (post-qualifying exam) in recruiting advertisements placed by British legal recruiters. For this reason, compared to U.S. firms, paralegals in other countries tend to be less commonly used and are for the most part an innovation introduced by Americans.

Without a law degree it is difficult to compete with junior lawyers—at least in the UK. It is difficult to understand why the use of paralegals is not more common worldwide. Paralegals are profit centers for law firms. Paralegal work is charged out at $45-100 per hour or more and the paralegals are paid significantly less on an hourly basis. Since without employees to leverage lawyers quickly reach the limits of their earning capacity because there are only so many hours in a day, it is odd that the use of paralegals has not become more widespread. Nevertheless, the paralegal profession is growing because of its favorable economics and licensing is never an issue.

Paralegals can provide valuable services to foreign law firms. Native English speakers are used to review draft language. There are

also corporate opportunities available especially in the area of contracts and contract
management.

Chapter 3

RESEARCH

THERE ARE MANY "HOW TO" BOOKS and materials written about finding employment generally. Much of the information written about finding a job generally is applicable to the search for a job in the legal field. Go to the library and look at several of these books. It does not matter that the copies you review are the latest versions, what you want to do is get a feel for the process. Newer books will focus on the latest technologies but it is worthwhile to familiarize yourself to how jobs were found before the days of the Internet. Legal jobs are not yet posted on social media, though this is starting to change.

What Color is your Parachute? is a perennial favorite and frequently updated job hunting guide. There is no reason to purchase an updated guide; the information in the older editions is just as useful. The book contains tips and techniques that might give you an idea or help you solve a problem that comes up in your job hunt.

Chapter 4

WHERE TO GO?

WHERE IN THE WORLD SHOULD YOU work? The answer, all other considerations being equal, is where you can find employment. American lawyers have found employment in the Middle East. China has been a popular place for foreign legal employment but more so than in other places, Chinese language proficiency is often required. India has no shortage of lawyers and the Indian government seeks to tax worldwide law firm profits. You will see few opportunities for foreign lawyers in India. The 'stans are hotbed of oil exploration and exploitation and so there are legal jobs there as well.

But all sorts of different countries from time to time will appear on your radar. I have been contacted for jobs in places as diverse as

Papua New Guinea, Myanmar and Cambodia.

Chapter 5

FINDING A JOB IS A JOB

FINDING A JOB IS A FULL-time job. It is important to get organized and put in the necessary time. You need to have a place to work from. While it is possible to work from home this is not recommended. There are many distractions which will interrupt your work. The sound of barking dogs will be perceived by an employer as unprofessional if contact is made by phone during the day.

You should treat your job search as you would any other job. Your tools should be available and readily accessible–not stuck in a box somewhere. Appropriate office supplies should be at your fingertips and not require a special trip to an office supplies store. For your job search to be successful you must be organized. In addition to getting a day to a page calendar you will need bond paper so as to be able to print resumés. This may be obvious, but a resumé should be printed on bond paper and not copy paper. Get a day-to-a-page calendar and on each page write down the contacts you made that day. This will give you a sense that you are getting closer to your goal.

If you would prefer to do this digitally, go ahead. The key is to know who you talked to and on what day. Years ago, the science fiction writer Jerry Pournelle was also a columnist for Byte Magazine, a journal devoted to what was then the nascent field of information technology. In one of his columns, though it only tangentially had anything to do with computers, Jerry counseled keeping a paper log. Every single name, address, e-mail address and telephone number went chronologically into the log. Use a bound book with a day to a page format so no pages can get lost. Re-reading the log helps to bring to mind the means by which you got to a person and who that person was. Such a log is useful also in your law practice, especially when contacting large institutions. You may be shuffled from one department to another and unless you write down the names of these departments and the people who work in them it will be difficult to recreate whom you spoke with months or even years later. A job search log may not work for everyone but I highly recommend it.

You may get lucky and find that the first resumé you submit draws an interview from an employer. But unless that interview results in an offer which can be accepted you have nothing and must keep working. Each day should start with a to-do list in case the days starts to drag. Unpleasant tasks are best addressed early in the day. Not doing so gives you a chance to obsess on them and only produces further procrastination. Get organized using whatever system you like. Keep a daily record of the people you contact and each job application. There are two reasons for this—first, it will help you remember if you get a call out of the blue two months after you applied for a position on-line and you honestly remember nothing about the details of the position. Secondly, keeping a record makes follow-up calls easy. A calendar-based system works for many.

If you do not treat your job hunt as a priority it will remain only one of your secondary interests. If you want to find a position you must make an effort every single day. If you do so, the chances of finding suitable employment increase dramatically.

Job searching is a numbers game. For every ten contacts there will be one good lead. For every ten leads there will be one interview. For every ten interviews, on average, there will be one job offer. That is why looking for a job is a full time job itself. When I say that it is a numbers game I am assuming that you are applying for appropriate positions for which you are qualified. Sending in one resumé after another for positions that require credentials you do not possess is a waste of time and money.

Finding relevant jobs means doing research and following leads. Interviews can yield valuable information and referrals.

Sometimes a law firm that decides not to hire you may mention a client who needs an in-house lawyer.

Setting up contacts and writing letters all takes time. A canned or form letter will immediately be recognized as such and is unlikely to get a reply. A personalized letter will almost always draw a response.

Jay Foonberg is the author of *How to Start and Build a Law Practice*, one of the most-stolen books from law school libraries. First written long before the ubiquity of the Internet, Foonberg counseled using paper rather than the phone when making client contacts. Foonberg teaches that because paper is real and something must be done with it. Writing a response is one way to deal with paper. Moreover, paper gets seen. Someone is assigned to open the mail or direct the mail to the proper recipient. Directed mail is sent to a individual or a team who must deal with it. Paper documents are often kept in a file. Files are accessed from time to time. You never know who might see paper. While e-mails do get forwarded, often they are seen by only one individual sitting at a terminal. Locked in a digital file, your e-mail might as well not exist. It is so very easy to delete an e-mail (though, as we all now know, permanent deletion is something else altogether) while throwing paper away is a different story.

Any response from an employer is an opportunity. Even if the employer ultimately does not hire you, the contact has given you a chance to learn more about his practice areas and so to educate yourself about the possibilities of your employment in the field. The lack of an opportunity today may mean nothing three months from now. Business is ever-changing. You are changing. There may not be a need for your skill set today, but three months from now things might be different. Three months from now you will have more experience and that new person may be a more attractive candidate. I have had friends who applied at Saudi Aramco only to be rejected three times before finally being offered a position.

If you find yourself sitting at a desk with nothing to do after making all of your daily contacts and applying to all of the appropriate positions you could find, take the time to conduct research. Try another approach. If you have been favoring one web site over another, switch. Go back and try an approach you haven't tried in a while. Your action list is a guide for what has worked and what has not. Renew old contacts. Doing so will harm nothing and otherwise you will never know if their requirements have changed.

Talk to colleagues and see if they have any news which you might apply to your search. If you get your news from the Internet, look at a newspaper. And if you get your news from newspapers, take a look at the Internet. It is your responsibility to make something happen. The best way to find a job remains through a personal connection. You are but four to six degrees of separation from the job that you want. The website LinkedIn is based on this concept. To be successful, you must cast your network net as widely as possible.

You never know where information is going to come from. At a bar function you may meet someone who makes a suggestion about your search, since you should be telling everyone you meet that you are looking for a new position. Being referred to an employer is significantly more effective than just having your paperwork come in over the transom. The referral literally opens a door that was closed to you before. This is a record you should keep, if for no other reason than to thank the person who made the referral.

Chapter 6

JOB SEARCH BUDDIES

JOB HUNTING, LIKE LOSING WEIGHT, IS a lonely task. Some people hire a personal trainer to cajole them into the gym because they do not have the discipline to exercise every day. An exercise buddy who calls you up to remind you to exercise, an annoying person who demands only that you do what you should be doing is sometimes useful to have around. Alcoholics Anonymous will supply a sponsor for someone who is trying to stop drinking or avoid a relapse because it is not easy to achieve these goals by yourself.

There will be days when you are depressed and your job search seems hopeless. There are times when you get frustrated and sad and you don't want to look anymore. After applying for dozens of positions and being rejected each time, it is easy to want to give up and crawl into a cave.

There are times when you would rather put your feet on the table at home, make popcorn and watch television instead of working out. A job hunt buddy will help you keep focused. He will call you and ask, "how many resumés did you send out today?" He will make sure that you keep your eye on the prize. It is your job to return the courtesy and make sure that he does not give up either. It is useful to have that external pressure–the same pressure you would have if you were working.

Job-hunters can band together. Many cities have job hunting clubs where members can get together and share tips in an office-like atmosphere. Looking for a legal job may be a more competitive endeavor, but so is looking for any kind of job. It may well be that the person you choose to be a "job-hunt buddy" has qualifications similar to yours. Sometimes the two of you may be competing for the same positions. But it also means that if one of you is hired, he may be in a position to lend a hand later on. It also means that you have two sets of eyes looking for opportunities. He will—not may, but will—come across job opportunities that you have not found or which you may have seen but which somehow did not register. Similarly, you will come across job opportunities that will be more of interest to him. So you pass them along.

A job hunt buddy need not be a lawyer or even working in the legal field. Nevertheless, their job search may be complementary to yours. Your job search buddy is probably looking for a local job and is uninterested in working overseas. For him, passing along foreign jobs to you will be easy. Similarly, because you are looking to relocate overseas you will not be tempted to keep news of otherwise interesting local jobs to yourself. A job search buddy may come across places where there are law jobs that you had not considered. Not every employer is familiar with hiring attorneys because some employers have never hired an attorney before. So they advertise in inappropriate places. Rigzone is a site for oil patch professionals–drillers, engineers, roustabouts and the like. Nevertheless, from time to time you will see attorney jobs posted on that site. The chapter, *Book of Numbers* identifies similar job search sites.

Chapter 7

A RESUMÉ IS A CERT PETITON

ALAN DERSHOWITZ IS ONE OF THE most prominent attorneys in the United States. He first came to public notice for his successful appeal and defense of Claus von Bulow. Later, he was one of the attorneys who defended O.J. Simpson.

Several years ago, I defended a movie producer who had purchased the film rights to a biography of Bobby Darin called *On Borrowed Time*. The book was eventually made into a movie starring Kevin Spacey. Before Spacey acquired the rights, my clients became the subject of a criminal indictment because two of their investors had criminal pasts. The presence of mobsters in the dock overwhelmed the jury and they were convicted.

After their conviction, they were interested in hiring Dershowitz for their appeal. The Eleventh Circuit Court of Appeals had turned down their request for bond pending appeal. They asked me to speak to Dershowitz and see if he would be willing to take their case.

What to do? What you will read in the rule books is that if you are turned down at the federal appellate level, you can file a Petition for a Writ of Certiorari to the U.S. Supreme Court. The formal elements of the petition are described in the Supreme Court's rules. But what the rules do not spell out—and what Dershowitz told me—is that a Petition for a Writ of Certiorari is advertising. Though a certiorari petition looks like an appellate brief, it is not an appellate brief: if the writ is granted, you still have to write the brief. A certiorari petition is an effort to convince the Court to take your case. You write to get the Court's attention, to convince the justices why this case should be one of the only one hundred and fifty or so cases they accept for consideration each year.

What does this have to do with job hunting?

In the United States, the term for a short biographical document which is submitted as part of an initial application for a job is "resumé," even though the proper spelling is "résumé." In the rest of the world, the most common term is c.v., which is short for curriculum vitae. When applying for a job overseas, use the term c.v.

You should not have a single resumé. That is, you should have several. Create a base resumé with your vital statistics (date of bar admission, name of law school, year of graduation, undergraduate degree, non-legal job experience).

A generic resumé can be used for positions that are entry level or which do not require any experience. I suggest using a program like Scrivener or Microsoft's One Note to organize and contain the different resumé versions you will need as well as to keep your various drafts in one place. With this method, it should be easy to prepare a specific, tailored c.v. for a particular position within minutes and not hours.

Prepare different resumés in advance for different areas of the law which interest you. Then, when you see a job advertised, you will be ready to respond quickly and effectively. Your resumé should be a very formal, dry business exercise with no frivolity. Do not add any information about hobbies or interests–quite frankly, no one cares that you enjoy knitting or playing tennis. Instead, prepare an alternative resumé that contains information about your lifestyle, special interests and hobbies. You may never have an opportunity to submit it, but there may come a time when it is appropriate to do so.

There are many companies and resumé coaches who offer services in order to help you come up with the "perfect" resumé. These services can probably be dispensed with. Instead, study several samples of attorney and executive resumés to get a feel for them. A Google image search will turn up dozens. Of these, choose a design that you like.

For many advertised positions, resumés must be submitted on-line through a resumé-

building fill-in-the-blanks process. Online resumés also eliminate all of the formatting you
worked so hard on. The process emphasizes
the importance of key words when it comes
to resumé submission. If the job descriptions
outlines the need for an intellectual property
attorney, the words "intellectual property"
must appear in your resumé. If they do not,
the automated systems simply will not select
yours for review.

From the employer's point of view, the real
problem is finding the right person within a
deluge of resumés. For every advertised position, there will be dozens, or even hundreds,
of resumés submitted. Many resumés will be
grossly inappropriate for the position. People
will apply even though they have not read the
job description.

There is a good deal of controversy over
whether a resumé should be limited to one
page or not. Early on in the game, it is probably best to keep your resumé to one page
simply because it will be one of dozens—or
hundreds—and there may be several review-
ers who do not want to wade through multi-

page resumés. There is little advantage to a two page resumé. If your content will not fit on a single page, save the non-essential for the multi-page version.

For overseas positions, format your c.v. to fit A4 paper and test the results. Otherwise you may find that Microsoft Word has turned your one-page resumé into a two-page version. Letter paper is not used outside the Western Hemisphere.

There will come a time when a longer resumé is appropriate. So you should have both formats set up so you can produce a single page, a two page or even a multi-page resumé on a moment's notice. For highly paid executive positions, an employer in the middle to late stages of reviewing your candidacy will want to see more documentation. That is the time when you bring along or forward the longer document.

In the same way that a certiorari petition is advertising, your resumé is advertising. The single page resumé is advertising and you should treat it as such. You are not simply telling your story, you are writing copy.

While it is possible that you will be hired solely on the basis of your resumé, it is much more likely that you will have an interview, and perhaps a call-back, before getting an offer. Consider the resumé you bring along to that interview your appellate brief. That resumé does not have to be limited to one page. Make it as complete as possible. It does not matter if that resumé is five, ten or even twenty pages long. Of course, you will have a copy of your single page resumé with you as well.

An executive summary consisting of a single paragraph should begin the document. The most precious commodity these days is attention and there will be many who will not read even an entire page. They are too busy. Summing things up in a paragraph lets them engage in productive conversation with you even if they have not read your resumé in its entirety.

In addition to on-line resumé building, some on-line systems will require resumés to be submitted in Microsoft .doc format. Different computers will display .doc files

differently based on the defaults the user has
set, so you really have no way of knowing how
your resumé will display.

Another important issue to consider when
submitting a Word document is the need
to scrub the metadata hidden in the document.   There are several sources on the
Internet which describe how to do this.   In
the past, copying the entire document into
another Word processing program or text
editor and then re-importing the document
back into Word would remove metadata and
revisions. Caution must be exercised to en-
sure that this procedure has in fact stripped
the metadata.   There are various add-ons
as well which will insure that revisions you
made to the document are not transmitted to
potential employers. This is why you need
to be careful when using a single Word-based
document for your multiple resumés as there
is a risk that document revision histories will
be passed along. Your potential IP attorney
employer might wonder why you forwarded
a different executive summary highlighting
an internship at a litigation firm.

Learn to use international legal vocabulary. It's not "litigation" but "contentious matters". "Transactional" law may be a term you use, but also consider "corporate/commercial". Do not assume that a foreign employer will understand acronyms that you take for granted. It is not sufficient to spell out unfamiliar acronyms, you have to explain the nature of your work. This is not necessary for a U.S.-based employer. There is some familiarity with an acronym like FCPA since the Foreign Corrupt Practices Act is applied extraterritorially by the United States, but don't assume that anyone knows what ERISA is.

I once asked an American law firm to provide information about agency law in their state. I received a well written, but useless article about the principal/agent relationship. I should have used the word, "distributorship". In the international context, 'agency' usually refers to the appointment of a distributor or sales agent in a particular country. Many countries have rules governing these relationships to protect the local distributor. You cannot always assume that American legal vocabulary is understood overseas.

Foonberg's teachings about paper is important in this context as well. In most cases, because of time and distance, you will be forced to apply for overseas positions by e-mail. In appropriate cases, consider sending a copy of your paper resumé with a cover letter to the potential employer. The problem is that depending on location, a letter might take weeks to arrive, if it arrives at all. For letters to Europe, regular mail can be used. For the rest of the world, use Express Mail or DHL. DHL has much more of an international presence than other U.S.-based courier services. Express Mail will be cheaper. Remember that employers will immediately receive dozens of resumés upon the initial publication of a vacancy and many of those applications will be from people who are unqualified and who simply apply for every single posting. There will be no penalty and in fact there may be a slight advantage in having your documents arrive after the initial rush.

A resumé should be accompanied by a

targeted cover letter. A really good, tailored letter is often better than a resumé. Sometimes such a letter will draw a response asking for your resumé and then you know that the employer is interested. I highly recommend paper letters. Paper requires a response in a way that digital media does not. Paper gets attention. It demands action. It is so much easier to delete an email than throw away a letter. Letters tend to get answered. Given the current state of e-mail technology, you can never really know if an e-mail is received. Most know this, so following up e-mails to make sure they have been received is appropriate. On the other hand, if you are sending a letter domestically and it is not returned you are fairly sure that it has been received. Paper letters sent by courier will have a delivery confirmation. E-mails can be sent to the correct addressee and be dumped into a spam folder without human intervention. Because of these technological issues, using both methods at the commencement of a relationship may be the best alternative.

In this letter you should explain why you

are right for the position. Try to put yourself
in the shoes of the employer and explain how
you will be a valuable addition to the team.
For a law firm, you might mention that you
expect to make money for the partners. For
a corporation you might mention that by hiring you the company will be able to keep legal
costs down. Remember that you are writing
advertising copy. But do not try to sell what
you cannot deliver.

If you have some connection to the country where you are applying, whether due to
family or other reasons, mention this in your
cover letter. Be careful about possibly raising
taboo subjects. Politics and religion are subjects best avoided in a cover letter.

The "alternative c.v." I have referred to
above should not be sent prior to receiving
a request for an interview. In fact, I would
probably bring the alternative c.v. along on
the first interview, but I probably would not
use it. If you get a call-back, it might be appropriate to share the document depending on
the circumstances. Some interviewers want
to fill in the blanks and if you get a question

about hobbies it might be a good time to present your alternative resumé, or at least quote from it.

Finally, your resumé–actually your resumés–should be living documents. Keep them up to date. There may be nothing to add with respect to new employers, but you can list conferences attended, new studies or even freelance work you have done in order to keep your resumé up to date. A matter need not have been completed in order for you to be able to list it on your resumé. Even if you have done only part-time work on a particular matter, there is nothing wrong with listing these new experiences even though you have had little overall responsibility for them. As a new lawyer at a large firm it is unlikely that you would have a great deal of responsibility over anything but minor transactions or cases. The fact that you are able to perform real work and meet deadlines is itself an asset.

Unless you are seeking a job in academia, if you are more than five years out of law school your academic accomplishments are essentially meaningless. What is important is the fact of graduation, licensing and ex-perience. The identity of your law school is important because your school may have an active alumni association overseas and per-sonnel at your potential employer may have attended the same institution. Otherwise, the fact that you are an American-trained lawyer is what is crucially important. If you had the good fortune to attend a top-tier school by all means trumpet that fact. But even here you must be careful, since if you have had a lackluster career since graduating questions may well be raised.

Your resumé should contain no spelling or grammatical errors. Spell check the docu-ment. Print it out and review it again. Prop-erly spelled but misplaced words are hard to catch. "In apple a day" is obviously wrong but draws no squiggly red line alarms. Have another set of eyes proofread your resumé to help catch such errors.

Try to send out at least ten cv's each day, or make at least ten contacts each day. This is not that hard; though right at the beginning it might be difficult.

There is nothing wrong with writing some-one in the industry and asking for help. From time to time I get letters from young lawyers asking about their careers and I have put them in touch or tried to help them. It doesn't happen that often, but when it does, it is flattering. You may be surprised at the helpful responses you receive.

Some employers may ask to see a writing sample. There is nothing wrong with using a paper you prepared at law school. Indeed, academic papers do not carry a shelf-life and there is no reason you cannot use a good one even if it was written years ago. If the document is too old its conclusions may have become stale, but this is not really important. A document that heralded a new trend or addressed an issue thought to be on the cutting edge may have been overcome by events due to the passage of new laws or the issuance of new court decisions.

The reason why an employer has asked for a writing sample is not because of a keen interest in your musings about the necessity of reforming the nation's copyright laws but to see if you can write like a lawyer. You will be writing wherever you work; it is an important part of our profession as lawyers. A potential employer merely wants to know that you are up to the task.

If your certiorari petition is successful, you still have to write the brief and argue before the Court. If your resumé is successful, you still have to win at the interview stage.

Chapter 8

SOCIAL MEDIA

YOU SHOULD HAVE YOUR OWN WEB page which should contain your resumé. Just open your generic resumé in Word and then "Save as html". Remove your telephone number from your resumé unless it is a business number; camouflage your e-mail address to avoid spam or use a specialized e-mail address you have established for your job hunt. Any personal information from your resumé before you post it.

These actions will make your resumé discoverable on the Internet. This is not entirely a good thing and could create problems if one of the resumés you have submitted to an employer varies too much from what you have posted on the web. While each case will be different, perhaps it would be better to post contact information only.

You should do a background search of yourself to see what a potential employer may find. If there is derogatory information or information that belongs to another time, you may be able to take action to remove it. This may require going to court but you are a lawyer after all and preparation of a lawsuit should present no real obstacles. Do not forget about small claims court. Google does business in every state and so can be sued everywhere. While the dollar amount which can be awarded by a small claims court is limited, many small claims courts have the power to grant injunctive relief. If you want information deleted from a website you should be able to sue the web site owner, obtain a judgment and an order requiring Google to remove offensive material. How to do this in a specific case is beyond the scope of this book, but it is important to note that you are not without remedies if someone has made inappropriate posts about you.

An e-mail address should be appropriate for the business environment. Nicknames and what you believe to be cute references are inappropriate. It is unlikely that an employer would look for potential candidates on Twitter, but if you are under consideration for an appointment it is likely that an employer will check your reputation on various types of social media. Make sure to scrub these to the extent that you can.

It is an act of kindness to provide a reference for another person. The problem is that being a reference for someone can be work. A reference may not respond immediately because he wants to write something appropriate and unfortunately he never finds the right time or the right mood to write. Faced with a deadline, he sends a response that is adequate but not optimal.

When a company wants to alert the press about a new product, they make it easy for them by sending along a press release containing information about the product. Do the same for your references? When you ask someone to do this favor for you, make it easy for them. Send along a draft paragraph which they can use when asked about you. It is much easier to correct or add to some reference text than to draft something original. Don't go overboard in your praise of yourself. Your reference text should contain no derogatory information and should confirm a fact that is already listed on one of your resumés.

If you ever applied to the Florida Bar or for a U.S. Government security clearance you are already familiar with how references are handled. Investigators assume that the names of people you have given as a reference will do nothing but sing your praises, so they are for the most part ignored. These first-level references are usually asked only for the names of at least three other people who know the candidate. The investigators then discuss your background with these second-level references. The potential for mischief is enormous because your reference may not be someone you know too well. Or the reference may be someone you used to know well but who doesn't know that you were in a divorce and that suggesting the name of an ex-father-in-law is probably not a good idea. Reduce your exposure by providing your references with the names of three references. These three should be provided the names of the first-level additional references. This can easily be accomplished by sending all of the references a proposed text, just like a press release.

Chapter 9

THE OFFICE

WHERE YOU WORK FROM DURING A job search is important. As tempting as it is to work from home, try to resist the temptation. Rent may be cheap since there is no added expense. The problem is that a certain amount of human contact is required for a job hunt to be successful.

Working from a coffee shop like Starbucks can be problematical. A coffee shop is noisy. There may be free Internet but contacts are awkward. Is someone saying hello because they want to help you in your job search or because they want to chat with an attractive woman? You can afford interruptions from the former, but not the latter (although feel free to disagree with me on this point). There may not be barking dogs—though even this is not assured—but it will be difficult to take a business call because of the noise, especially if that call is from overseas. Even given modern telephony, under the best of circumstances, you are lucky to hear 75% of an overseas call. Throw in an unfamiliar accent, cultural differences and the hesitancy involved when speaking with a new person and you are likely to have a suboptimal experience. A serviced office will provide a much more business-like experience.

There are business incubators for lawyers. There are lawyer-landlords who lease out an office within their law office. Finding one of these on a month to month basis should not be difficult and there may even be some part-time work available to keep yourself afloat while you continue your search.

If you cannot find a place with other lawyers, you could get a virtual office for at least one day each week. Regus is probably the best-known company in this sector and they offer virtual office services. The privacy of a serviced office can be useful for your job search. If you can afford to keep the office you have a place to receive mail, send faxes (remember the paper rule), and have more space to lay out papers or organize files. At home you have to deal with the mess and the annoyance of family members disturbing files.

If you can get an office it will be easier to look for work. The second reason is because Regus and places like it are business incubators. New businesses are the primary source of new jobs worldwide. Someone at Regus down the hall from you may need your services. Sometimes they may ask you to do a little job for them and the cash helps you keep things afloat while you look for a permanent position. Or they stick their head into your office and mention that a client is hiring. Or a business they do business with. You may even decide you like freelancing and the time you spend job-hunting becomes less and less.

Chapter 10

NETWORKING

TAKE ADVANTAGE OF ALL OPPORTU-
NITIES for networking. There are bar association functions, organization functions,
continuing legal education, groups for young
executives and alumni associations. There are
events at every jurisdictional level, whether
state, federal, county or city. In larger cities
there are more foreign associations and many
more opportunities for foreign networking.
Organizations like the Council on Foreign Relations frequently sponsor programs. There
are foreign embassy or consular receptions.
Universities sponsor talks or lectures open to
the public. There are many possibilities. All
of these opportunities should be put to use.
Unfortunately, only a few of these will have
anything to do with the practice of law in a

foreign country. Still, you never know what a contact might lead to. A foreign client may be interested in employing a U.S. lawyer for a period and your new contact has no one in the firm to send. You simply never can tell if a new contact can aid in your search so do not dismiss the possibility out of hand.

Sometimes simply learning of the commencement of a legal project may provide a reason to connect. Countries use consultants to help them rewrite laws to make their economies more competitive.

There are several federal agencies with a presence overseas, but there are also entities which operate at a state or local level in an effort to win foreign business or learn more about foreign markets. Organizations like the Bilateral U.S.-Arab Chamber of Commerce in Houston and other state foreign trade offices conduct their own programs and are generally valuable resources.

Being a lawyer means knowing how to interview people in order to obtain facts related to a case. An interview for a job is no different. Sometimes you interview just to get information about the industry or to make contacts. This is called the informational interview. It may not lead to employment with the company interviewed, but the information obtained may help you get a job somewhere else. Case in point: one of the best interviews I ever had was with Pan American Airlines. They basically laughed at me. I said, "Do I have any chance of getting a job here?" They said, "No." So I asked, "Do you know of any airline that's hiring?" They said, "Why don't you try Mexicana?" So I went to Mexicana, told them that I had been referred by Pan Am, and the next day got the job.

Chapter 11

DO AN EMPLOYER A FAVOR

JOB CANDIDATES OFTEN FEEL THAT POTENtial employers are doing them a favor by appointing them to a position. From the employer's point of view, though, you are solving a problem by offering to take a job. From an employer's view, finding a capable employee who can competently fill a vacancy is cause for celebration. Job searches can take a long time. Unqualified candidates and time wasters are a drag on business.

It is important to maintain a proper attitude and not get discouraged. When you offer yourself for a position there is someone on the other side of the table who desperately needs a solution. If you are that solution, you are doing him a favor. It is difficult to realize this unless and until you are in the position of having to hire someone. Work is piling up. You need help. When the new employee finally arrives, the employer's thought is one of relief.

What this means is that the attitude of "oh please hire me" is less than half the story. I cannot emphasize this enough. That does not mean that you should be arrogant but merely that your negotiating position is stronger than you think.

The transaction is not one-sided. I have been in the position of having to hire people and when you're in that position, it is much worse than being on the other side of the desk looking for a job. A couple of years ago I had to staff a satellite office at a government agency for the purposes of a project whose main purpose was the drafting of a legal code for a special jurisdiction from scratch. The agency wanted us to have one lawyer at the satellite office from 9-5 every day. We had no one we could send. I asked for junior lawyers from our branch office in Dubai, but the request was met with resistance. We "solved" the problem by manning the office in shifts, but the government agency was unhappy with that less than optimal solution. If a competent attorney had walked into the door, I would have been thrilled to employ him. Opportunities do in fact exist and many come up unexpectedly. To get these positions you have to be in the right place at the right time and that is but a question of luck.

Chapter 12

IN THE PAST

IN THE PAST IF YOU WERE looking for a law job overseas there were few resources. You could check the international volumes of Martindale-Hubbell and get the names of foreign firms, their addresses and telex numbers. I suppose from time to time it was done, but I have never heard of anyone sending in a job application by telex. Determining whether or not a foreign firm had any openings was next to impossible. For many years this was the starting point for what would become a local search upon arrival in your new home. The coming of the Internet has meant the death of distance. It is now possible thanks to the existence of tools that simply were not imagined years ago to locate foreign law firms and companies without leaving home. Thanks to e-mail, round-trip communication that would have taken a minimum of two weeks can now be effected within minutes.

It is easy to read foreign newspapers on the Internet, but it is still difficult to read foreign classified job ads. Fortunately, their use has declined drastically. In addition to Google and other search engines, there are job vacancy aggregators which list hundreds of foreign jobs. Simply finding one of these listings had heretofore been extremely difficult. Today it is trivial. For that reason, there are few reasons why you should not expand your job search to include foreign employers.

A few newsstands sold foreign newspapers and it was possible to purchase Sunday editions on the off chance that there might be a few attorney jobs listed. Newspaper classified ads are not used much any more and they were rarely used for attorney positions anyway.

It is now possible thanks to the existence of tools that simply were not imagined years ago to locate foreign law firms and companies without leaving home. Thanks to e-mail, round-trip communication that would have taken a minimum of two weeks can now be effected within minutes.

It is easy to read foreign newspapers on the Internet, but it is still difficult to read foreign classified job ads. Fortunately, their use has declined drastically. In addition to Google and other search engines, there are job vacancy aggregators which list hundreds of foreign jobs. Simply finding one of these listings had heretofore been extremely difficult. Today it is trivial. For that reason, there are few reasons why you should not expand your job search to include foreign employers.

Nevertheless, looking at ads (or job postings in the Internet age) that are at least six months old is useful. Why? When a new ad is posted, hundreds of people apply. Many of the people who apply do not even have remotely appropriate qualifications. I once posted a job at the University of Miami School of Law. I was looking for a researcher. I got an application from someone who was working as a cook. He never mentioned that he was even a law student. Now, multiply this on a large scale. You are the employer, you post an ad, you get hundreds of responses. You may even have filled the position and the person just didn't work out. When you're on the verge of posting again, a previous candidate follows up with the credentials you are looking for.

One of the problem with these tools is that because they are automated, a job listing with a misspelling will not be discovered in a search. When dealing with foreign companies, even words like "lawyer" are sometimes misspelled and so never appear in search results.

Simply getting names of firms is not enough. There are few law local or regional firms that are the size of U.S. or UK mega-firms. The law in foreign countries in many cases remains a family business. Without some kind of connection, it will be difficult getting your foot in the door. Fortunately, many foreign firms recognize the value of having a common-law trained, native English-speaking attorney on staff. The advent of globalization means that firms that once had an entirely local practice must pay attention to foreign clients, foreign counter-parties and transactions in English. Having a Western lawyer makes even these small family firms more competitive in a global economy. Once hired you will be a valuable addition to the local team.

Chapter 13

INTERVIEWS

IF YOUR RESUMÉ HAS DRAWN INTEREST, an interview will be scheduled. This may be anything from an ad-hoc unscheduled phone call to a more formal video conference. If you are working through a recruiter, the recruiter will arrange for a telephone or video interview. You may get a telephone call from the law firm or company asking to arrange a video interview.

A video conference conducted with an employer overseas may use Skype or another software conferencing system. Install Skype now and become familiar with it so that you are ready if an employer calls. The day of a video conference is not the day to install new software. Doing so always means last minute technical issues. Sad experience teaches that it is prudent to have a land line or mobile telephone close by in case your Internet connection goes down or in case latency makes the use of Skype impossible.

While video conferences are useful and extremely economical, if there is any way you can get a live, in-person interview try to do so. This will not only give you the opportunity to see the employer's premises but it will give you an opportunity to meet people who would not otherwise be participating in a video conference. It is also easier to sell yourself in person than it is in a conference or over the telephone. This may be impracticable because of costs, but volunteer anyway. Sometimes company personnel travel to the United States or easily accessible third countries where an in-person meeting can be scheduled. The importance of a face-to-face meeting cannot be over-emphasized. A favorable first impression will go a long way in securing the position you desire. If there is any way to get a face-to-face meeting, try to do so.

Chapter 14

DRESS LIKE A LAWYER

IF YOU EXPECT TO BE TREATED like a lawyer, dress like a lawyer. This means conservative business suits, for both men and women. This is what you wear to an interview. The only exception is an interview held on a Saturday. Lawyers do not wear suits on Saturdays. So on that day alone you are permitted to wear a sport coat. For women, a jacket and pants is still the norm.

In the Middle East, the weekend is Friday-Saturday and not Saturday-Sunday. Since Friday is the day for more formal religious observance, lawyers are unlikely to be in their offices on Fridays but may go to the office briefly on Saturdays, just as in the West.

Chapter 15

NO LOCAL LICENSE NEEDED?

ONE OF THE MOST PERSISTENT MYTHS about practicing overseas is that you cannot do so without bar admission and bar admission is next to impossible. Most countries still restrict bar admission to their citizens. The Commonwealth is an exception.

The fact that bar admission overseas is not a requirement to practice overseas comes as a surprise to many, especially those who have just spent three years to qualify to take a state bar examination. American bar admission rules are a patchwork and from state to state are very difficult to reconcile on any principled basis. Because the idea of working overseas as a lawyer without being admitted locally so goes against the thinking of most new lawyers, it is useful to review national standards to see just how fluid they are and why such overseas practice is nothing different conceptually from an in-house attorney, admitted in one state, who gets transferred to another.

American state bar admission is for the most part national, because of the American Bar Association law school accreditation requirement. Immediately after admission the practice becomes ferociously local. Nevertheless, bar examiners in most states are happy to admit non-local attorneys who have not stepped foot inside their state as long as they have practiced for at least five years in another jurisdiction. It is not clear how practicing for five years in Georgia will qualify you to practice in New York unless the practice of law is truly national. Though we are ruled by a single Supreme Court, the practice of law in the United States remains local.

A foreigner walking into any courtroom, whether federal or state, in any state in the United States is usually shocked both by the lack of practice uniformity from jurisdiction to jurisdiction as well as the overt preference shown to local attorneys. Outright discrimination is often voiced against non-local attorneys and the rules determining who is a non-local attorney are not alway intuitive. A Miami attorney who travels to Ft. Lauderdale for a court proceeding in Broward County can expect to hear comments about "Miami attorneys" from the bench, despite the fact that the "Miami attorney" may live and vote in Broward county and only commute to an office in Miami. An attorney with a home in Morristown, New Jersey but an office in Manhattan can be expected to be heard railing against "New Jersey attorneys" in arguments in Federal District Court in Manhattan. In Illinois' Cook County courts, attorneys from Wisconsin may as well be from Mars despite the fact that not a few Chicago attorneys have cabins or vacation in Wisconsin.

In many states, judges are elected. Their political campaign funds come from the attorneys who practice before them. Other countries consider this a corrupt practice. The reason why judges favor local attorneys is because local attorneys can both donate and vote for them while non-local attorneys can only donate. Savvy firms with a caseload in "foreign" counties often take the precaution of contributing to judicial campaigns to insure a level playing field.

One would think that this prejudice against foreign attorneys would not be the case with federal judges, since they are appointed for life and need not stand for election. But this is too often not the case either. Federal judges are many times selected from the state bench, where they have learned to discriminate against non-local attorneys. If they have not sat on the bench before they will learn from their colleagues who have. Practicing attorneys used this xenophobia tactically in their practice.

Even so, one would think that federal practice would be a more friendly environment for today's mobile attorney. The basic qualification for employment as a federal attorney in a federal agency is bar admission in at least one state. There is no requirement that the new hire be qualified to practice in the state where the federal job is located. Attorneys can transfer within the agency to a position in a different state with no difficulty.

When a federal job is more political, such as that of U.S. Attorney, there is often a requirement that the prospective candidate be admitted to the local bar. But this is not always the case. As in the case with other U.S. administrative agencies, an attorney may move to another position in the Department of Justice or be assigned to a different jurisdiction without being qualified to practice in that state.

The former Strike Force within the Department of Justice was a unit primarily focused with prosecuting racketeering and organized crime. Its attorneys were sent all over the country in aid of this mission and frequently they did not have local bar admission. Under the rules of every single district court, Department of Justice attorneys in good standing are entitled to admission to practice.

Otherwise, the rules are a patchwork. Admission to the Eastern District of Michigan requires payment of a fee and admission in at least one state, not necessarily Michigan. Florida Bar membership is a prerequisite for admission to the bar of the Southern District of Florida. The late Morey Sear, a federal judge in New Orleans, once even went so far as to claim that federal agency attorneys were not practicing law while working for their agencies. Bar regulators who impose sanctions on such attorneys when they misbehave have a very different view.

In theory the federal courts are national courts but in practice they are just as local as any other jurisdiction. The seal used in all the federal courtrooms is the same except for the name of the district. In 1938 the Supreme Court said that there was no such thing as "federal common law" and the process of legal unification started during the Civil War was slowed. A knowledge of the federal rules will get you in the door but without knowing the particularities of local practice you may find yourself in trouble.

There is little uniformity among the local districts when it comes to routine matters such as the filing of motions. In New Jersey, attorneys in criminal cases customarily file a letter memorandum with the presiding judge in lieu of a motion. The letter is addressed to opposing counsel and sent to the Clerk of Court where it is made a part of the court file. Failure to follow this procedure will draw an invitation from Chambers to conform your practice to local customs. Follow the New Jersey practice of sending a letter memorandum to a judge in the Southern District of Florida and you will be rebuked for attempting to correspond with the judge. Pointing out that the procedure is different in other districts will only raise eyebrows. The local judge is most unlikely unaware of the practice in other districts, for not only does each district—and there are ninety-four of them—have its own local rules, each judge will also have his own private, unpublished rules which need to be learned and followed.

For all these reasons, the mindset of most practicing attorneys in the United States is ferociously local. The world of business is anything but local. Even though every business has its own local roots, the minute the business owners consider re-incorporating in Delaware or establishing a subsidiary out of the country for tax reasons the perspective becomes a global one. Even though the United States has only been dragged kicking and screaming into the global marketplace, most companies are quite happy to accept a foreign customer's order and ship his product. Some stragglers remain. Usually telling a U.S. company that you need a SWFT number because you need to pay by wire transfer will only draw a blank. Telling a company that you prefer to be paid by wire will similarly summon a host of excuses as to why this is inconvenient or "not according to policy." Even global companies that should know better fall into the American "we are the world" local trap. Tell Ford Credit you want to pay an invoice by wire transfer and you will be told that this method of payment is only available to foreign retailers. It is no wonder that the cross-border fluidity of Bitcoin has made the digital currency so popular. Get a job as an attorney with Ford and you can be based as one of Ford's assistant corporate counsel in any State in the Union. Twenty years ago, all you needed to do to work in-house was to maintain bar membership in a single jurisdiction. While you could not go into court except on a *pro hac vice* basis to represent the corporation, this option was nevertheless available and the company works with outside counsel for court appearances anyway. For transactional and other corporate commercial work, the single State bar admission was enough.

Today almost all states have provisions for limited bar admission for corporate counsel admitted in one state but based in another. There are several requirements for such out-of-state in-house admission and the right to regularly appear in court is usually not granted.

American states also grant limited bar admission to foreign attorneys who limit their practice to advising clients solely on matters of foreign law. To a great extent, this is fantasy. There may be several reasons why a Venezuelan company might contact a Venezuelan attorney based in Miami who is not admitted in Florida, but if that company wants advice on Venezuelan law there is no shortage of competent counsel in Caracas.

Why go to Miami? The obvious reason is because the Venezuelan company wants advice on local U.S. requirements and unless it can find a U.S. admitted attorney in Caracas, it has to go to the source. So to think that a Venezuelan attorney in Miami in such circumstances will exclude any mention of U.S. business law in the context of giving advice to the Venezuelan client is simply naive. While it turns a blind eye to this reality, one of the reasons why the organized bar started providing foreign legal advisor licenses to foreign attorneys was to have some basis for attorney discipline, because otherwise these attorneys worked outside the organized bar's regulatory framework . Roughly three-fifths of American states will reciprocally admit attorneys who have practiced law for at least five years and can show some familiarity with local rules. The five years must be spent in the licensing jurisdiction. States' rules are not uniform with respect to the treatment of an attorney who is admitted in one state yet who has spent the bulk of those five years in a different jurisdiction. To my knowledge, there is no physical presence test.

Vacation states like Florida are exceptions to the reciprocity rule. There is really only one state that can make the argument that a specialized study of its laws is a legitimate practice requirement. That state is Louisiana, since its legal system is not based on the common law. The reciprocity rules which obtain in the rest of the states strongly suggest that the official position of the Bar in these states is that the practice of law is not that local at all.

If you get a job in a law firm in an American jurisdiction where you do not have a license, at some point you will be expected to qualify. This is not the case overseas.

The bottom line is that in the business world, the issue of bar admission functions only as an initial disqualifier. If you are not admitted to practice anywhere you will not be able to obtain a position as in-house counsel. Overseas, you will not be able to get a job as an attorney–or "legal consultant"—unless you have been admitted to at least one jurisdiction. In the United Kingdom, it is possible to take an attorney's examination to qualify if you care to do so. Otherwise, you can work as a foreign solicitor without any difficulty.

A few countries from time to time attempt to rein in foreign attorneys practicing on their soil. Since these attorneys do not appear in local courts regulation is done at the level of national immigration. Because consultants have become so widespread, the position of the legal consultant who is licensed only in his home jurisdiction is commonly recognized. The words "attorney" or "lawyer" whose use is usually a third rail which will call down the wrath of foreign bar regulators.

When you are practicing overseas you are still subject to the ethical rules of your licensing jurisdiction. Your presence overseas is irrelevant. There are some interesting conflict of laws situations which might come up, but in years of practice overseas I have rarely encountered them. What is more common is when a country specifically passes a law to limit the effects of an American law.

Otherwise, as is the case with Baker & McKenzie and many other firms, American lawyers routinely practice overseas as consultants and are never formally admitted to the local jurisdiction.

Chapter 16

HOW TO GET EXPERIENCE

ONE OF THE MOST VEXING PROBLEMS facing a candidate is meeting a prospective employer's experience requirements. Recent law graduates will bemoan the fact that without experience they cannot be hired and without being hired they cannot get experience. This complaint is misplaced, for the law is perhaps one of the most facilitative environments for obtaining experience outside the formal confines of employment. If you lack experience in an area, you can obtain it easily enough. It is true that certain kinds of experience will be more difficult to obtain than others. But even experience that is relatively difficult to obtain is nevertheless available for lawyers.

The practice of law can be separated into

two general areas. There is the practice of ideas and the practice of actions. The practice of actions–taking depositions, defending motions, appearing at motion calendars, picking a jury, trying a case–is one in which an attorney physically interacts with a tribunal. Several elements are needed for this interaction to occur: you must be admitted to practice, there must be a controversy, you must have a client and a matter must be the subject of a hearing or proceeding in court.

Even trial lawyers with decades of experience were once lawyers who had never been inside a courtroom. Usually Big Law firms do not permit their young associates to go into court by themselves. Instead, these lawyers begin their litigation careers writing memoranda, doing research and assisting more experienced lawyers before being allowed to speak on behalf of a client on their own. Even firms which have a reputation for providing a good deal of trial experience for young attorneys do not let recent law graduates pick juries or try cases without first having sat second chair several times under the tutelage of a more experienced lawyer.

The lack of trial experience is certainly an initial barrier which may keep some jobs out of reach. You can nevertheless make yourself a more attractive candidate by structuring your own apprenticeship outside of employing institutions: you can get experience at the courthouse itself.

There are many ways to accomplish this. Solo practitioners cannot be in more than one place at a time and often need assistance with motion calendars and the like. Sometimes solos will send secretaries to cover a calendar call. Judges greatly dislike this practice because secretaries or paralegals are not admitted to the bar and so cannot bind a client. Offer to help out one or more solo practitioners–especially without charge–is the kind of offer that often gets accepted. Even though motion calendars may seem trivial, they are nevertheless formal court proceedings and court etiquette must be followed. Handle a few and you will become more relaxed about appearing in court. A solo may let you appear on an uncontested motion because he is in trial. Start handling a few of these and before you know it you will have a good deal of courtroom experience–at least, you will have that courtroom experience analogous to a litigation associate at a large firm who is not permitted to appear in court on his own.

Involvement in more complex matters is also within reach. There are legal aid institutions in many cities or your local bar association may sponsor legal aid programs for the poor. Volunteering to represent indigent individuals in small claims cases in order to get trial experience.

Small claims cases are best because your goal is to gain experience in order to permit you to find employment overseas. Because some people are chronically litigious, normally small claims cases end with trial.

While small claims cases are tried without a jury they are trials nonetheless. Judges will relax the rules for laymen, but have no doubt: if your opponent is a corporation it will have to be represented by a lawyer and the presiding judge will expect professionalism. The judge will know that you are a young lawyer and will insist on proper trial procedures, etiquette, the marking of exhibits, not asking leading questions of a witness on direct and the like.

Under no circumstances should you accept a federal criminal appointment. Once accepted, it is very difficult to disentangle yourself from such a case and federal court calendars trump all others. Your need to resign from a case due to a pending move overseas may be denied. This is unfortunate, since otherwise federal court is an excellent place to learn how to try a case. Even small criminal cases can stretch out for a year, and you want to find a new job and be able to move on.

In a few months you will have sufficient courtroom experience to keep pace with other recent law graduates. Every case you work on can be added to your litigation resumé.

Appeals fall within the practice of actions but court appearances are very limited. Usually there is but a single hearing. The rest of the work falls within the scope of the practice of ideas. Busy trial attorneys always need appellate help. They do not need assistance arguing their cases before the court of appeals–that they find easy to accomplish. After all, an appellate argument is just another hearing. Preparing a brief means writing a book and this takes a very different skill set than making arguments in court. It is especially difficult to find the time for considered academic reflection amidst a heavy hearing schedule, not to mention the time required to draft the brief, and the additional time required to make sure the brief conforms to the court's rules.

The second type of law, the practice of ideas, covers writing and research. Law firms have associates. Judges have law clerks. It is a time honored tradition for young lawyers to gain experience researching and writing for older lawyers. The fact that you do not have a job as an associate or a law clerk does not mean that you are barred from doing writing and research. You have a computer; law libraries are readily accessible. Writing and research means experience. Nothing stands in your way from getting that experience.

There are many audiences for writing and research. Experience in these areas is much more easy to obtain because the participation of third parties is seldom required. Today, more so than perhaps at any time in the past, it is easy to write and obtain an audience for your work.

Intellectual Property law is one area of the law where there is a good deal of international commercial activity. Nevertheless, up until relatively recently, this subject was rarely taught in law schools. Copyright and patent law was an elective backwater.If you wanted to learn copyright law you checked out *Nimmer on Copyright* from the library and that pretty much was it. No longer a backwater, for the past thirty years IP has and will remain a "hot" area of the law.

Commercial attention paid by American companies to intellectual property has made this area of the law extraordinarily dynamic. Confidential information,trade secrets–all of these areas are cutting edge. So how do you get experience in this area? *Write an article.*

Do the research and write.

Newspaper reporters are assigned articles by their editors even though they have no particular experience in the subject matter. But they learn. They do research, they report. You are in a much better position than they are to write about legal subjects. Being admitted to the bar means that your state has certified that you are competent to handle every kind of legal matter imaginable. There are but a few exceptions, such as death penalty cases. Certainly you are skilled enough with your law degree to research a topic and produce a report.

As a young associate in a law firm, this is the type of work you would be assigned. The only difference is that in doing general research and writing you are not advocating one position over another, but conducting a survey of the current status of the law. If a reporter can write an article about an unfamiliar topic, certainly a young lawyer can write a survey about an unfamiliar legal subject. In fact, young lawyers are particularly suited for this task. Because you have recently taken the bar exam you will at least have a passing acquaintance with most areas of the law. Because you are a lawyer, you know how laws are made, how different laws can complement each other and how laws can become inoperative when found unconstitutional.

One of the principal dividing characteristics between big and small law firms is the quality of their precedent libraries. Some firms might call this their forms library and other firms may not have one at all, relying solely on documents created by individual attorneys for individual matters which may or may not be shared with others. There is even a difference amongst Big Law firms. Freshfields Bruckhaus Deringer, one of the UK "Magic Circle" law firms, has a precedents library worthy of envy. Forms for just about any legal matter conceivable have been digitized and automated to give their attorneys a solid starting point for the next transaction or matter. Yet when the Dewey, LeBoeuf firm went bankrupt, the firm's international precedents library was not even considered a firm asset in the partnership bankruptcy.

The law firm's physical books were listed and valued, but the much more valuable precedents library was ignored. The Bankruptcy Trustee claimed that the library was merely work product and had no value. Freshfields, I think, has a different view, as do many other firms within the world of Big Law.

The monetization of a law firm's intellectual property is one subject that you can address (please let me know if you write on this topic). There are dozens of matters you could write about in this field–and in every other field. If you are stuck for a topic, pull law review articles that are ten years old and bring them up to date.

Twenty years ago I wrote an article about taking depositions abroad. I am aware of one law review article, itself now more than ten years old, that addresses the subject as well. Surely there have been new developments in the field. Even if nothing has happened other than to confirm conclusions reached years ago, that in itself is valuable information. If you cannot think of an original topic, find an older law review article and bring it up to date in the light of recent cases. Such an exercise has value for anyone with an interest in the subject.

You can address federal subjects from the point of view of state law, and state law from the point of view of federal law. You can write on international subjects, extraterritoriality, procedural rules for international arbitrations or any other subject area where you lack experience. Currently there is much interest in the extent to which American courts should pay attention to developing foreign legal standards. There is also interest in the U.S. government's efforts to enforce domestic laws overseas. Tomorrow there will be new subjects to write about.

After writing your article, submit it and publish it. In addition to law reviews, there are trade and specialized legal publications that are hungry for content. List the articles you have written under "Publications" on your resumé. Even if you have had no success publishing your article, you can publish it on Amazon, Docstoc or other sites. There are many sites on the Internet which explain how to do this.

Writing need not be limited to preparing articles about different areas of the law. Localizing forms or modifying old forms based on recent case law can be useful. These can be posted on your web site. A potential employer might find them, but find them or not, they can be listed on your resumé.

As a bonus, many states give continuing legal education credit for writing books and articles. In this manner, you can get experience in a field in a way that is not open to other professionals. Your lack of experience can be remedied through hard work. The only limits on your reading and writing is your dedication and the time you have available.

I am not suggesting that writing is easy, but much of your professional work overseas will consist of writing in one way or another. Writing articles or short books is good practice for the work you will be doing overseas.

In the past, getting an advanced degree was often suggested to assist those who otherwise lacked experience. There is nothing wrong in obtaining an advanced degree, but a certificate in another field may be more useful. I am not in favor of an LL.M. for an American lawyer seeking to work overseas unless you study taxation. You already have a doctorate. Another legal degree is just lagniappe. Getting any kind of accounting certification will be useful, even if it is not a CPA. Similarly, engineering experience is useful.

Programs leading to a certificate in Project Management—a field that barely existed thirty years ago—are also very helpful. There are short courses in business and accounting. The one day "Accounting for Lawyers" continuing legal education classes may whet your intellectual curiosity but will not qualify you to be a bookkeeper. Formal junior college accounting classes will, and they will be of great use down the road. Any certificate that is legitimate, business-related and can be obtained in less than a year is worthwhile.

Because you are a lawyer, the problem of no experience is not a problem at all. Your licensing jurisdiction has faith in you to handle any matter. There are substitutes for obtaining different kinds of experience. No one will expect you to run a million dollar deal at the outset. If you do not have experience in a particular area, do not despair. That experience is within your reach. If you see gaps in your resumé because of a lack of experience, go out and fill them.

Chapter 17

OFFICE POLITICS

OFFICE POLITICS ARE A FACT OF life. It is often said that the smaller the institution, the greater the political in-fighting. Assuming that you do not know anyone at your potential employer's, you are a neutral candidate. There will be those who already work at the company who want to hire a relative or a friend. If you think that nepotism does not exist, think again. If you think that Caroline Kennedy's daughter won a coveted internship at the *New York Times* because of her extraordinary journalistic skills, you might also consider that her last name might have had something to do with it despite The Times' loud denials. Weeding out questions of ethnicity, hiring you neither rewards nor punishes any hidden special interests at the company. Do not do anything which would disqualify yourself from consideration.

There is a great Pilipino word for "troublemaker" which is derived from Spanish. The word is *contravida*, and it means a person who is "against life." Each office will have one, and maybe more than one. Your resumé and your candidacy will probably not be reviewed by a single individual. At some point, the *contravida* may get ahold of your resumé and seek to derail your candidacy because of resentment that a cousin or a friend was not hired. Or maybe the troublemaker wants to use the office as a dating service and thinks that only cute males or females should be hired. There is no limit to possible pettiness. If your references get strange telephone calls or e-mails let your contact at the firm know. These might be wholly innocent but they might also be the work of a *contravida*.

In one case, a troublemaker mounted his own personal investigation of a candidate that was more thorough than a CIA background investigation. The job candidate learned of the ad hoc investigation when he was getting repeated inquiries from the same company with inane follow-ups. It turned out a trouble-maker did not want a new hire at all and so decided to try to derail the job-seeker's candidacy. There is no real solution to all of these machinations. Knowing that they are under-way and reporting them is one way to deal with them. Otherwise you can only act pro-fessionally yourself. The last thing you want is to be drawn into a political battle before you are even hired. On the other hand, the existence of intense infighting might suggest that it is better to look elsewhere.

Chapter 18

BOOK OF NUMBERS

FISHERMEN IN THE GULF OF MEXICO used to keep personal notebooks containing Loran C numbers to identify waters rich with fish. For a day of successful fishing, a fisherman would motor to the coordinates listed in the notebook because at that location plenty of fish had been found before. Gulf fisherman each had his own jealously guarded book of numbers which was never shared with anyone.

The following list is not unlike those books of numbers. The focus is primarily on the Middle East because that region hires the more English-speaking attorneys than any other. I share these numbers with you with the advice that fisherman have successfully fished these waters before. That does not mean there will be fish at every location. Sometimes a site will yield poor fishing. The market changes and new jobs are posted all the time; it is important from time to time to revisit sites that previously had not been fruitful. In conducting your own searches you will identify your own numbers; places that are particularly good fishing for you.

While a successful foreign job search can be conducted with just these numbers alone, consider these numbers to be a starting point. Your own research will turn up other places that work better for you. These numbers are particularly weak in Africa, India, Australia and South America. Fishing in those waters is more difficult.

Craigslist Caution

Start with Craigslist (craigslist.org). After identifying your destination country, post a blind ad stating that you are an attorney seeking employment. You may receive one or two good responses and for that reason placing such an ad is worthwhile. Unfortunately, most of the responses that you receive will not be from employers but from clients who need an attorney. About a third of these will be the type of client who does not need really need an attorney but a Don Quixote to take charge of a lengthy and fruitless crusade. It goes without saying that such a client will feel so strongly in the merits of his case that he will try to convince you of the cause's inherent worthiness. Indeed, his cause will be, at least in his mind, so worthy that you should agree to take his case without they payment of any fee.

Others will be those sad individuals who have already gone through two or three lawyers and have found only disappointment in the courts. They too will want you to pick up their cudgel. While these individuals may be willing to pay attorneys fees they will expect you to win a result different from that obtained by the two or three attorneys to whom they owe money and who have already worked on the case. Leave these clients alone. There will be no cooperation from previous counsel because the client severed the relationship before settling his account. Getting files from previous counsel will be difficult. If such a person owns a company and is willing to appoint you the company's general counsel and one of your duties will be to handle what is always a non-company related personal case, that might be a different story but understand the minute there is bad news to report on the personal case your general counsel position is out the window. Offer to refer such individuals to other lawyers, you will generally find that the client/employer has already spoken to most of them. Unfortunately, that is the nature of attorney classified advertising.

Lemontree is the United Kingdom's equivalent of Craigslist and is worth a look as well. Craigslist is not everywhere. Other countries have their own active bulletin boards.

Aggregators

1. http://totallylegal.com This is a legal job search aggregator. It primarily lists positions

in the United Kingdom but other foreign jobs are frequently posted.

2. http://indeed.com Indeed.com is another job search aggregator. You can target your searches by country; for example, to search for positions in Qatar go to qa.indeed.com; Kuwait, kw.indeed.com; Saudi Arabia, sa.indeed.com.

3. http://www.bullhornreach.com/ Bullhornreach is a site where recruiters post open positions. As of this writing, their search function is being upgraded so it might be worthwhile to use Google with the search limiter "site:bullhorn
reach.com" when trying to find jobs on this site.

4. http://jobs.thelawyer.com/ The Lawyer is the United Kingdom's legal weekly for the profession. The site contains many United Kingdom and foreign job listings.

5. http://Rigzone.com Rigzone is a site for the petroleum industry with a very active job board. Overseas law and contract jobs are frequently posted.

6. http://oilcareers.com Similar to Rig-

zone, this site contains foreign law and contract positions in addition to other oil sector
jobs.

7. http://jobline.acc.com The Association
of Corporate Counsel has an active job board.

8.   http://usajobs.gov While this is the
general U.S. government job site, foreign
positions do get posted from time to time.

9. http://unjobs.org/ and http://un.org/en/em-
ployment/. These are two web sites which
contain listings of attorney positions at the
United Nations around the world. The first
site is a private site which contains listings of
non-governmental and other international
agency jobs as well.

10. http://fircroft.com Fircroft is an aggregator for technical jobs but many overseas legal jobs are posted.

11.   http://LinkedIn.com While LinkedIn
is not a job aggregator per se, many jobs get
posted here. Consider using a different language LinkedIn for a different focus and to
see different submissions.

12. http://www.monster.com Monster.com
is worth a look; sometimes there are for-

eign job postings on Monster's U.S. site but this is not Monster's bread and butter. You might have better luck with one of Monster's foreign sites. To reach them, open an anonymous page (using an "Incognito" window in Google Chrome or a "Private" window in Firefox and try to reach this page: http://www.monster.com/geo/siteselection. This page will let you select among Monster's many foreign sites.

Recruiters

The Advocate Group	www.advocate-group.co.uk
Bespoke Professionals	bespokeprofessionals.com
Blue Pencil Legal	bluepencil.co.uk
Cameron Cole International	camcoleinternational.com
Footprint Legal	footprintlegal.com
FSR Search	fsrsearch.com
Gulf Talent	gulftalent.com
J Legal	jlegal.com
Cuff Jones	cuffjones.co.uk
Cypress Recruiting Group	cypressrecruiting.com
Law Connexions	lawconnexions.com/Jobs.aspx
Lawyers in Private Practice	lawyersinprivatepractice.com
Leap 29	leap29.com
Lila Crose Legal	lilacroselegal.com
Matthew Peters Int'l.	mp-i.com
Nexus Legal	nexuslr.com
Open Door Recruitment	opendoorecruitment.com
Michael Page	michaelpage.ae
Propel Consult	propelconsult.com
Douglas Scott	douglas-scott-co.uk
Talent Partners	talent2.com
Taylor Root	taylorroot.com

Other Resources

China

http://www.asialegalblog.com/
http://www.chinalegaljob.com/
http://www.hughes-castell.com.sg

http://www.hughes-castell.com.hk

Japan

legal-intel.com

Kazakhstan

http://www.bolashak.com: This is a recruiter for jobs in Kazakhstan.

http://www.tengizchevroil.com/careers/vacancies: This is a joint venture hiring in Kazakhstan.

Another: http://www.ncpoc.kz/vacancies.asp?LangID=3

Saudi Arabia

http://www.jobsataramco.eu/: For its size, Saudi Aramco has a tiny legal department and exclusively uses White and Case as outside counsel. Nevertheless, the company has been assigned non-oil related work by the Saudi government and has contract positions available from time to time.

South America

Bumeran.com is a job board. Add the two letter Internet country code to access the local board for the country you seek, i.e., Argentina: bumeran.com.ar; Colombia: bumeran.com.co; Mexico: bumeran.com.mx; Peru: bumeran.com.pe; etc. For Bolivia there is trabajopolis.bo.

Craigslist is also useful for initial contacts in South America.

Don't Forget

No matter your views on politics or whether or not the United States should be a global policeman, the fact is that the U.S. military has been active overseas since the country's foundation. There are overseas attorney jobs in the military. Active duty military service may not be your cup of tea but you may find it is a worthwhile beginning for your overseas legal career.

The U.S. State Department is responsible for the conduct of foreign relations and operates a diplomatic corps called the Foreign Service to fulfill these responsibilities. These are not legal jobs per se but your legal education is good preparation for them.

What is not as widely known is that other agencies, especially those with law enforcement responsibilities, also maintain an active foreign presence and foreign attorney jobs from time to time are advertised. The Drug Enforcement Administration and the U.S. Agency for International Development are two agencies of many with foreign positions. So it is a good idea not to restrict your U.S. Government searches solely to the Departments of State and Defense.

Chapter 19

PLAN B

THE DAYS OF YOUR JOB SEARCH quickly turn into weeks and the weeks into months. How long will your job search take? Market conditions will change. New laws and new markets mean new opportunities. The Al-Gosaibi bankruptcy case in Saudi Arabia attracted platoons of attorneys and a hiring push not only in the Middle East but in the United Kingdom as many law firms thought there would be a great deal of litigation and boots on the ground were needed. Though the Al-Gosaibi case did not ultimately lead to as much legal work as was originally thought, the global financial crisis of 2008 is still spawning new cases.

You need to have a Plan B if your job search fails to produce results in three months. Some suggest that a good alternative is to go "all in" and simply move overseas to your dream destination. Some have done so successfully, while others have failed.

You cannot travel to Saudi Arabia without an invitation unless you are a Muslim, and even then it's somewhat tricky because you would need to make sure you had enough time after *umrah* to travel to Riyadh for meetings. You can travel to the Emirates, Bahrain or Lebanon without any visa issues, but you are going to have to commit to $3000 or so in expenses before you meet your first contact in person. If you can do that, fine, but most American law students seeking internships cannot. And you are then only giving yourself three months to arrive, identify and secure a position before you have to leave. It might be more useful to make one or two targeted business trips to your regions of interest to meet with recruiters and to try to line up interviews. Yet since most of this–except for meetings with recruiters–can be accomplished at home, it is much more economical not to go unless you have an interview in hand.

If you want to work in a particular country, it is possible that you can do so without even ever having visited. Before moving to a place you should make at least one visit for the purpose of familiarization. There is much that you cannot learn or accomplish on the Internet. At some level, though, a job search must be financed. Unless you are independently wealthy you must have enough money to pay for your telephone, Internet, postage and all the bills attendant to daily life. What should you do in the meantime?

Freelancing is one idea, especially if doing so earns you experience or makes you more competitive. Working in a related field might be useful. You can do a great deal of freelance work for other lawyers. In addition to handling minor court appearances, there is always a need for memoranda, document review and all other kinds of legal work. There are jobs, such as contract management (sometimes called "contract engineers") which you are qualified for because of your legal degree, even though a law degree is not required. A familiarity with FIDIC (the French acronym for the "International Federation of Consulting Engineers") is helpful and FIDIC guides are available on the Internet and in the library. You can also teach business law or criminal justice on a part-time or substitute basis.

In the meantime you can devote at least some of your foreign job search efforts to finding a job locally. While a law degree in the United States is no longer neither a guarantee of employment, jobs can still be found. How to find a legal job in the United States is outside the scope of this book, but a good deal of the advice will be useful for a local job search as well.

Chapter 20

SHAMELESS PLUG

DON'T FORGET TO TAPE THE TOILETS is an employment orientation manual for Saudi Arabia and Bahrain. A Canadian law firm opened an office in Al Khobar, the Saudi province connected to the Kingdom of Bahrain by a land bridge. The book is published by Andalus Publishing and they asked if I would mention that book here.

So I have done so.

Don't Forget to Tape the Toilets is a useful manual for those who are going to work in either Saudi Arabia or Bahrain but it is not about practicing law in either country. Perhaps Andalus will come out with another book that addresses that deficiency.

Chapter 21

ABOUT THE AUTHOR

SIDNEY KORSHAK IS AN AMERICAN-TRAINED attorney who has worked overseas for many years.

Index

www.ingramcontent.com/pod-product-compliance
Lightning Source LLC
Chambersburg PA
CBHW020838210326
41598CB00019B/1943